BORIS NEMTSOV, 1959–2015: SEEKING JUSTICE, SECURING HIS LEGACY

HEARING

BEFORE THE

COMMISSION ON SECURITY AND COOPERATION IN EUROPE

ONE HUNDRED FIFTEENTH CONGRESS

SECOND SESSION

FEBRUARY 28, 2018

Printed for the use of the
Commission on Security and Cooperation in Europe

[CSCE 115–2–1]

Available via www.csce.gov

U.S. GOVERNMENT PUBLISHING OFFICE

28–910PDF   WASHINGTON : 2018

For sale by the Superintendent of Documents, U.S. Government Publishing Office
Internet: bookstore.gpo.gov   Phone: toll free (866) 512–1800; DC area (202) 512–1800
Fax: (202) 512–2104   Mail: Stop IDCC, Washington, DC 20402–0001

[II]

BORIS NEMTSOV, 1959–2015: SEEKING JUSTICE, SECURING HIS LEGACY

FEBRUARY 28, 2018

COMMISSIONERS

WITNESSES

APPENDIX

BORIS NEMTSOV, 1959–2015: SEEKING JUSTICE, SECURING HIS LEGACY

February 28, 2018

COMMISSION ON SECURITY AND COOPERATION IN EUROPE

WASHINGTON, DC

The hearing was held at 3:32 p.m. in Room 138, Dirksen Senate Office Building, Washington, DC, Hon. Roger F. Wicker, Chairman, Commission on Security and Cooperation in Europe, presiding.

Commissioners present: Hon. Roger F. Wicker, Chairman, Commission on Security and Cooperation in Europe; Hon. Benjamin L. Cardin, Ranking Member, Commission on Security and Cooperation in Europe; Hon. Christopher H. Smith, Co-Chairman, Commission on Security and Cooperation in Europe; Hon. Jeanne Shaheen, Commissioner, Commission on Security and Cooperation in Europe; and Hon. Cory Gardner, Commissioner, Commission on Security and Cooperation in Europe.

Witnesses present: Zhanna Nemtsova, daughter of Boris Nemtsov; Vladimir Kara-Murza, Chairman, Boris Nemtsov Foundation for Freedom; and Vadim Prokhorov, lawyer for the Nemtsov family.

HON. ROGER F. WICKER, CHAIRMAN, COMMISSION ON SECURITY AND COOPERATION IN EUROPE

Mr. WICKER. If it seems that Senator Cardin and I are rushing, it's because we have a lot to do in an hour. Senator Cardin and I have a series of votes that begin at 4:30. I don't know if any House members are expected today, but Senator Cardin and I will have some brief comments and then we'll get to our witnesses.

We're turning our attention in today's hearing to the loss of one of Russia's great democratic reformers, Boris Nemtsov, who was gunned down within sight of the Kremlin three years ago yesterday. Although the triggermen were apprehended and tried for their crime, the masterminds behind it have never been identified. Our witnesses today are people who knew Boris Nemtsov well. I stood behind them yesterday at the ceremony to rename a section of Wisconsin Avenue as Boris Nemtsov Plaza. I am very pleased that this hearing will focus on the legacy of Boris Nemtsov as Russians prepare to cast their votes in another presidential election next month.

We are honored to have his daughter, Ms. Zhanna Nemtsova, join us and reflect on her father's work and the prospects for realizing his dream of a free and democratic Russia. Ms. Nemtsova is joined by someone who is no stranger to members of the Helsinki Commission nor in the halls of Congress, thanks to his tireless and courageous work for democracy in Russia. Mr. Vladimir Kara-Murza knows better than almost anyone about the intense and all-too-often lethal pressure being applied to brave Russians like him and Boris Nemtsov, who engage in opposition politics. Mr. Kara-Murza directed the documentary film, "Nemtsov," a truly remarkable tribute to Boris, which opened in Nizhny Novgorod, and was screened in Moscow, St. Petersburg, and Washington, where many people in the room had a chance to see it. We're also very fortunate to have Mr. Vadim Prokhorov, the lawyer for the Nemtsov family, who's worked for years now to see the masterminds of this heinous act brought to justice.

As I mentioned, yesterday our witnesses participated in the naming ceremony for the Boris Nemtsov Plaza. As an American, I'm proud that Washington held the very first such official memorial of Boris Nemtsov anywhere in the world. The Russian people should know that we will continue to build legislative monuments to their heroes here, until stone monuments can be built in Russia.

Let me offer a word about the posters on display at the front of the room. They serve as a reminder that brave Russians have gathered on a regular basis to ask for justice for Boris Nemtsov. The photo of these flowers at the site of his murder could have been taken virtually any day in the past three years. Despite being removed every day the flowers are always replaced by the many people who revere the memory of Boris Nemtsov. I think these people deserve to be recognized for their devotion to democracy in Russia, and for their dedication to honoring one of Russia's great democratic leaders.

I'll place the rest of my statement in the record and recognize my colleague and dear friend Senator Ben Cardin of Maryland.

Senator Cardin.

HON. BENJAMIN L. CARDIN, RANKING MEMBER, COMMISSION ON SECURITY AND COOPERATION IN EUROPE

Mr. CARDIN. Well, first, let me thank our Chairman, Senator Wicker, for calling this hearing. Senator Wicker's been one of the great champions in the United States Senate on human rights. And we're very proud of his leadership here on the Helsinki Commission. And it's very appropriate that we have this hearing in regards to Boris Nemtsov.

I just really want to put this in context, Mr. Chairman, if I might. And that is, in Russia Mr. Putin uses an asymmetric arsenal of weapons in order to control his country, to oppress his people, and to interfere with the democratic principles of countries in Europe, and, as we've seen, in the United States in our 2016 elections. So this is a pattern of conduct. And I mentioned that we issued a report, and Damian Murphy of the Senate Foreign Relations Committee is here. He spent a year of his life writing this report on Mr. Putin and what he does in Russia, and the tools that he uses to compromise our way of life.

He uses his military. We know that. We saw that in Ukraine. We see that in Georgia and Moldova. He uses financing of fringe parties. We've seen that in several countries, including France, financing a coup in Montenegro, cyberattacks in the United States, misinformation in Germany and the U.K., support for fringe groups, including corruption—he uses corruption of his oligarchs in Russia in order to finance his own operations, but then gets involved in corrupt enterprises in other countries, as has been documented in Italy and elsewhere, uses energy as a tool, which we saw, again, in Ukraine.

I mention all that because he also uses murder. He also uses intimidation against his own people. And Boris Nemtsov was a victim of that violence. And it's very appropriate that we have this hearing.

Mr. Chairman, I recall how Boris joined me for the screening of "Justice for Sergei" in November 2010, and almost immediately after was assaulted at the airport upon returning to Russia. He helped us in getting justice for Sergei Magnitsky, who was also a victim of Mr. Putin's violence in Russia. So this is not an isolated example. We have not yet had justice for Mr. Nemtsov.

We know that the gunman who shot four bullets into Mr. Nemtsov's back served as a commander in the Chechen security forces under leader Ramzan Kadyrov, a close associate of Vladimir Putin. And while the gunman and his accomplices have been punished, the masterminds behind the assassinations have not been served justice. And I'm very pleased that we have our good friend Vladimir Kara-Murza here. Not once but twice they tried to poison him. And he's still here, and we're proud about that.

My final point is this: Many of us have been very outspoken about our opposition to what Mr. Putin has done to his own people, to democratic countries in Europe, his interference in the Middle East, in Syria, his support for Iran, and his attack here in the United States. But let's make it clear, we're on the side of the Russian people. And we very much want to acknowledge the brave Russians who have stepped forward to try to return Russia to a country that respects the rights of all of its citizens.

And following our chairman, I'll put the rest of my statement into the record and look forward to hearing from our witnesses.

Mr. WICKER. Thank you very much, Senator Cardin.

Ms. Nemtsova, you are going to be recognized first. We were delighted to hear from you yesterday at the Boris Nemtsov Plaza naming ceremony, and we're delighted to hear from you today. So please proceed.

ZHANNA NEMTSOVA, DAUGHTER OF BORIS NEMTSOV

Ms. NEMTSOVA. Thank you, Mr. Chairman, members of the commission. I would like to first of all thank you for holding this important and timely hearing, and for the opportunity to testify before you today.

As I have already said, it has been three years since my father, Boris Nemtsov, was gunned down on Bolshoi Moskvoretsky Bridge in the shadow of the Kremlin walls. And for three years, the official investigation has failed to shed light on the circumstances of the most high-profile political assassination in modern Russia.

Yes, the perpetrators were quickly found, detained, put on trial, convicted, and sent to prison. But two key questions remain unanswered.

The first is the motive behind the murder of my father. The investigative team and the court were silent on this. In Russia and across the world, politicians and experts and the general public understand that it was a politically motivated murder aimed at stopping my father's activities in the Russian opposition. The headlines that ran just after his murder read, "The most outspoken critic of Vladimir Putin was killed in Moscow."

Why don't the Russian authorities admit that this brutal murder was politically motivated? The answer is clear: If they recognized this, they could no longer say that the real opposition leaders—and I want today to stress the word "real," meaning those not dependent upon the Kremlin and its orders—are not repressed. In other words, they would have admitted on the official level that Russia is a country where the state engages in repression of opposition activities, from imprisoning to torturing to murdering political opponents. And this would, of course, have drawn a clear line between the permitted opposition that is allowed to criticize the authorities to a certain extent—for example, who pretend to be Putin's competitors in the upcoming presidential election—and the so-called non-systemic opposition that is outside of the Kremlin's control, and that not only advocates for democratic values but actually does real work, like publishing investigative reports on grand corruption in Putin's elite, as my father also did; those who lead mass anti-government protests, as my father did; and those who aspire to win the support of the majority of Russians, as my father did.

On several occasions I filed applications to reclassify this murder as the assassination of a political leader and statesman. This effort has not brought results so far, though even from the formal point of view my father was a member of the Yaroslavl regional parliament at the time he was killed.

The second question that remains unanswered concerns the organizers and masterminds of the crime. Not a single organizer or mastermind has so far been found and brought to justice, not even low-level people from Chechen leader Ramzan Kadyrov's inner circle. They enjoy the protection of the Russian state, and we have to bear in mind that this cover-up is a crime in itself. The reluctance to bring the organizers and masterminds to justice is very concerning. It seems that the authorities are either afraid of Kadyrov and his 30,000-strong army—if we presume that Kadyrov is the ultimate mastermind—or it is a combination of fear of Kadyrov and an attempt to hide something—for example, the direct involvement of Russian secret services and top-ranking Russian officials in the murder. And this lack of information is the best grounds for speculation.

If the Russian state is interested in proving that Putin holds no direct responsibility—and they are insistent on this—why don't they allow a transparent and impartial investigation that can help end the speculation? They have all the legal tools to do so, since there is a separate criminal case on the organizers that can be acted upon at any time.

In the past three years the Russian authorities have tried to erase the memory of my father and to end the public debate concerning the low quality of the investigation. They have failed. They have failed in part because of the international attention to this case and the recently launched special report at the Parliamentary Assembly of the Council of Europe.

Today I am asking you to help launch a similar procedure at the Organization for Security and Cooperation in Europe. And I strongly believe that this can help at least to reveal some of the details and to compel the Russian Government to react.

Thank you.

Mr. WICKER. Thank you very much, Ms. Nemtsova. We very much appreciate it, as we appreciate your attendance at the memorial yesterday.

The chair now recognizes Mr. Kara-Murza for his testimony. You are welcome, sir. Welcome back.

VLADIMIR KARA-MURZA, CHAIRMAN, BORIS NEMTSOV FOUNDATION FOR FREEDOM

Mr. KARA-MURZA. Thank you. Thank you, Mr. Chairman. It's good to be back.

Chairman Wicker, Ranking Member Cardin, Senator Shaheen, Senator Gardner, thank you for holding this important hearing and for the opportunity to testify.

As you just mentioned, Mr. Chairman—and, of course, you were there with us yourself—yesterday afternoon the family, friends, and colleagues of Boris Nemtsov gathered here in Washington for the unveiling of the world's first official memorial to him. By a law enacted in the District of Columbia, the block in front of the Russian Embassy in Washington was designated as Boris Nemtsov Plaza. This decision followed earlier initiatives here in Congress, and I want to take this opportunity to thank members of this Commission who had supported them: you, Chairman Wicker; Senator Shaheen; Senator Rubio; Senator Gardner; and Representative Cohen. Thank you.

It is a sad reflection on the situation in our country that the first official commemoration for a Russian statesman was held in the United States. But what happened in this city yesterday is important for many people in Russia. It is important for those who continue to hold remembrance marches, as thousands did again this past Sunday; bring flowers and candles to that bridge where he was killed; and stand guard over that unofficial memorial. It is important for people who continue Boris Nemtsov's work by exposing government corruption, by taking to the streets to protest Kremlin abuses, by speaking the truth about Vladimir Putin's regime. It is important for those who continue to believe in and fight for a democratic Russia. It is an affirmation that you can kill a human being, but you cannot kill what he stood for.

For the past three years, the Russian authorities have fought the memory of Boris Nemtsov almost as hard as they had been fighting him. They blocked all public initiatives for commemoration, removed the signs installed by private citizens, repeatedly destroyed the makeshift memorial on that bridge, the photograph of which you have here in this room. But last week, as we were preparing for the unveiling of Boris Nemtsov Plaza in Washington, the Moscow city government announced that it is reversing its position, and that it will now allow the installation of a memorial plaque on the apartment building in Moscow where Boris Nemtsov lived. They have apparently realized how it looks when the U.S. capital is honoring a Russian statesman while the Russian capital is refusing to do so.

Just as international involvement can help with the efforts to honor the memory of Boris Nemtsov, so it can with ending impunity for his killers. It has now been three years since the Russian opposition leader was assassinated on the bridge in front of the Kremlin, yet none of the organizers or masterminds of this crime have been identified or prosecuted.

Last summer, the Moscow District Military Court convicted five people as perpetrators in the murder. The man convicted of pulling the trigger, Zaur Dadayev, was an officer in the Internal Troops of the Interior Ministry of the Russian Federation, serving in the Chechen Republic. Despite numerous requests by Zhanna Nemtsova and her lawyers, Dadayev's top superiors—the head of the Chechen Republic, Ramzan Kadyrov, and the commander of the Interior troops, General Viktor Zolotov—were not even formally questioned by investigators. The chairman of Russia's Investigative Committee, General Alexander Bastrykin, has twice vetoed attempts by his subordinates to indict a Kadyrov associate, Ruslan Geremeyev—also an officer in the Internal Troops—as an organizer in the assassination.

In a deliberate gesture, the Russian authorities have refused to classify the assassination of Boris Nemtsov, former member of Parliament, former regional governor, former deputy prime minister, and, at the time of the murder, leader of a political party and regional legislator, under Article 277 of the Russian Criminal Code, as "encroachment on the life of a statesman or a public figure," instead choosing Article 105 that deals with common murder.

As state prosecutor Viktor Antipov told the court on July 25, 2016, and I quote, "We cannot allow for the murders of opposition members to be qualified under Article 277."

During the trial, the discussion of motive was largely absent, with questions relating to political reasons behind the murder repeatedly disallowed by the judge. Without questioning the obvious persons of interest, without identifying the motive, the organizers or the masterminds, the Russian authorities have declared this case, quote, "solved." What they want now is to turn the page, forget, and move on.

Please don't let them. Under our membership in the Council of Europe and the Organization for Security and Cooperation in Europe, Russian citizens are afforded the protections of international human-rights mechanisms. In May of last year, the Parliamentary Assembly of the Council of Europe appointed a special rapporteur with a mandate to review all aspects of the Nemtsov case. Today we are asking you to initiate a similar process under the auspices of the Organization for Security and Cooperation in Europe and its Parliamentary Assembly and to engage these mechanisms to conduct official oversight over the Russian legal proceedings, to shed light on their failures, accidental or deliberate, and on their political constraints, not to allow the Russian authorities to forget and move on, and to bring us closer to the day when all of those who had ordered, organized, and carried out the assassination of Boris Nemtsov are brought to justice.

Thank you very much, and I look forward to your questions.

Mr. WICKER. Thank you very much.

And attorney Prokhorov, you are now recognized.

VADIM PROKHOROV, LAWYER FOR THE NEMTSOV FAMILY

Mr. PROKHOROV. Mr. Chairman, members of the Commission, thank you for holding the hearing and for the invitation to testify.

The official investigation of Boris Nemtsov's murder by the investigative committee of the Russian Federation and the subsequent judicial procedure deserve serious criticism.

The Russian authorities are categorically refusing to recognize the fact that Nemtsov was murdered for his political activities. The investigators and the Moscow District Military Court have rejected almost all applications submitted by the lawyers of Zhanna Nemtsova, me and Ms. Olga Mikhailova, in particular the applications to reclassify the crime under Article 277 of the Criminal Code of Russian Federation as "encroachment on the life of a statesman or a public figure." The prosecution was brought under Article 105 of the Criminal Code, "Murder"—as in the cases of, for example, domestic murder out of jealousy, murder for commercial reasons, et cetera. Meanwhile, the authorities have failed to officially identify the motive behind the murder of Boris Nemtsov.

Five suspects were charged with the execution of the crime. All of them are natives of Chechnya, and some of them are close to Ramzan Kadyrov, the leader of Chechnya, and his entourage. The law enforcement agencies have not managed to detain any of the organizers or masterminds of the murder, and only some of the actual perpetrators have been detained.

There is no doubt that the traces of this crime lead at the very least to the inner circle of Ramzan Kadyrov, and maybe even higher. We have requested a number of investigative actions; in particular, the interrogations of Ramzan Kadyrov; the brothers Adam and Alibek Delimkhanov; the director of the Federal National Guard Service, General Viktor Zolotov; and others. The head of the investigative group has rejected almost all of our requests, and the courts have also refused to satisfy the complaints of the victims in this case.

During the jury trial at the Moscow District Military Court between October 2016 and June 2017, over 80 court sessions were held, dozens of witnesses were examined, and the case file amounted to over 95 volumes. At the same time, the victims were refused an opportunity to cross-examine a whole number of witnesses, including Ramzan Kadyrov and members of his inner circle. The court further refused to call General Viktor Zolotov, in whose command both the defendant, Zaur Dadayev, and his immediate superior, Ruslan Geremeyev, were at the time of the murder. In addition, General Viktor Zolotov was the longtime head of Vladimir Putin's personal security service and member of his inner circle. The presiding judge rejected a number of questions put before the witnesses by the victim's lawyers. Most of those questions were aimed at identifying the organizers and masterminds of the murder.

On June 29, 2017, the jury convicted all of the defendants. On July 13, the court sentenced them to long terms of imprisonment, from 11 to 20 years. However, there are doubts with regard to the guilt of at least one of the defendants, Khamzat Bakhayev, as the prosecution has failed to present any evidence against him.

On October 10, 2017, the Supreme Court of Russia has rejected the victim's appeal, as well as the appeals of the defendants.

We believe that there has been a breach of the right to a fair trial for the following reasons:

>the inadequate classification of the crime;

>the failure to officially identify the motive behind the crime;

>only some of the perpetrators have been brought to justice;

>none of the organizers or masterminds have been identified or prosecuted to date.

The problem is not that the identification of suspects is difficult or impossible. Our principal concern is that the investigative authorities are not willing to make any effort to do so. We believe that this has been decreed to them by the official Russian authorities.

In January 2016, the Investigative Committee separated the case against the unidentified organizers of the murder from the main case. The only individual named in this case is Ruslan Mukhudinov, a driver, whose whereabouts also remain unknown. We are not aware of any meaningful actions taken by the investigators under the separated case since January 2016.

There is an imperative need to draw international attention to this issue. Unfortunately, we have a limited choice of legal tools to push the Russian authorities toward further steps aimed at investigating the assassination of Boris Nemtsov, but such tools are available.

First and foremost, they are available within the framework of the international organizations of which Russia is a member, including the Organization for Security and Cooperation in Europe and the Council of Europe.

In addition, I am asking Western political leaders, public figures, diplomats, and journalists, when they are meeting their Russian counterparts, to ask them every time about the failure to identify the organizers and masterminds of Boris Nemtsov's assassination. This must become an embarrassing issue for the Russian authorities internationally. This is the only way to move the case forward.

Thank you so much.

Mr. WICKER. How hard is it to embarrass the government of Russia, Mr. Prokhorov?

Mr. PROKHOROV. It seems to me that it's very important to try any real steps to make this an embarrassing issue for them. And they are very sensitive to the real attention paid from the official international organizations—for example, by the Parliamentary Assembly of Council of Europe, by the OSCE, and so on—because they have no real answers to the question, where are the organizers and masterminds? And what's the problem to identify them when you have such powerful secret services and powerful authority in your country?

Mr. WICKER. Mr. Kara-Murza, let me ask you—if you'd like to follow up on that, that's helpful, but also to what extent is this case talked about throughout the Russian Federation? How widely is it known? Is it discussed in the print media? Is it discussed on the internet? Is it a matter of news? So if you could explain to us how what we're saying today and how the statement we made yesterday is disseminated, and help us understand to what extent this has gotten down to the grassroots of the Russian people.

Mr. KARA-MURZA. Thank you, Mr. Chairman. There is this dichotomy between the official picture that is created and maintained by the Kremlin's propaganda machine, by all of the state TV channels—all the national TV channels are now controlled by the state—and what's happening on the level of citizens and society. You know, for so many years the image that was put forward by Kremlin propaganda was that everybody in Russia loves and supports Vladimir Putin. And nobody cares about or supports the opposition.

I remember when Boris was killed and when we had his funeral, the line of people—the line of Muscovites, who came to say their goodbyes stretched for miles, from the Yauza River to the Kursky railroad station, all the way down the Garden Ring for two or three miles long, and not all people even had time to say their goodbyes because we had to move on. And every year, including just this past Sunday, February 25th, thousands of people walk down the streets in Moscow, and many other cities and towns in Russia— often despite the official bans on such demonstrations and rallies— to commemorate and to honor and to remember Boris.

And, of course, as you mentioned yourself, that memorial—that unofficial memorial on the bridge has lived on for more than three years now. I was on that bridge about an hour after Boris was killed and there were already the first flowers there on the ground. People were already beginning to bring the flowers. And those flowers are there to this day, every day, despite the fact that several times—more than 70 times during these three years—the Russian authorities, the Moscow communal services with the help of the police, have come to destroy and pillage that memorial. The following morning, the flowers and the candles reappear. So the popular memory of Boris Nemtsov very much lives on.

And those few remaining media outlets in Russia that have independent editorial control, that are not dependent on the state, in all of those media the main story yesterday was the first official commemoration for Boris Nemtsov in the world, the unveiling of Boris Nemtsov Plaza here in Washington. Actually, even state television felt compelled that they had to say something about it. Of course, half of what they said were lies, but that's the usual situation. Usually it's more than half. So I guess you could say that's a good thing. But even they had to mention it. So this is the kind of the contrast, I would say, that we have between what Russian citizens and what Russian society feels and the manipulated story that is presented in the official government media.

And on your previous question, if I could comment very briefly, I do agree with what Vadim has said, that it is important to make this issue an issue of public attention and public embarrassment for the Kremlin. And I think what is also important is to introduce some sort of international accountability for the people involved. We know that this is a pale substitution for the real justice that needs to be done. But there is now—thanks to you and your colleagues in this Congress—there is now a mechanism that introduces a personal measure of responsibility for people who are engaged in these types of abuses.

Two of the individuals that we have been talking about here today, General Alexander Bastrykin and Ramzan Kadyrov, are now designated by the United States Government as human rights abusers under the Magnitsky Act. We have, of course, here the original cosponsors of the Magnitsky Act, including the leader of it, Senator Ben Cardin. This is an absolutely crucial tool. In the absence of a real justice system in our country, this at least introduces some sort of responsibility for these people. It ends the impunity for these people. And as of today, there are now six countries in the world that have introduced their own versions of the Magnitsky Act. That's including the United States.

And of course, the substance of that measure is that if you are, after reaching a very high standard of proof, designated by a government of a country as a human rights abuser, you will no longer be allowed to enjoy traveling to that country, owning assets in that country, receiving visas from that country, using its banking and financial system. Again, this is pale substitution for real justice. Punishment for murder should not be an inability to open a bank account somewhere. You should be tried and sentenced to prison. But in the absence of such a possibility in our country, this is the least we can do. So we hope that the United States Government continues to use the mechanism of the Magnitsky Act, including in the context of the Boris Nemtsov assassination case, to introduce at least some measure of accountability for the people who are responsible for this.

Mr. WICKER. Ms. Nemtsova, let me just say how much I admire your dad. I met him some 21 years ago. He was first deputy prime minister. And I was there in a delegation led by Curt Weldon, representative from Pennsylvania, and Steny Hoyer, representative from Maryland. And I think our delegation, consisting of perhaps a dozen Americans, came away from that meeting so encouraged. We asked ourselves, is this the new face of the Russian leadership? And sadly, that was not to be.

I really thought, because of his prominence, he might be immune from assassination. Did you and your father ever talk about the possibility of this sort of assassination?

Ms. NEMTSOVA. Mr. Chairman, can I follow up on what the other witnesses have already said?

Mr. WICKER. You surely may, yes.

Ms. NEMTSOVA. Thank you. Because you asked an important question, whether we can embarrass the Russian Government. And I have clear evidence that we can. First of all, in 2015 I got an email from Anatoly Chubais. I don't know if you have met him. He was in the government, and now he's in charge of the state-owned company Rosnano, involved in development of high-tech products.

So, I got a letter from him. It was a big surprise. And he said: You shouldn't do three things. And one of them—one of the requirements was not to initiate an international investigation or oversight. And that's a clear sign that they're embarrassed. And when I got this letter I said, I will do all these things—directly opposite to what he said to me, not to insist on Ramzan Kadyrov's interrogation, et cetera, et cetera, to fire my lawyers. So I'm talking about this correspondence because it was made public by Anatoly Chubais.

Second, when we started this procedure at the Parliamentary Assembly at the Council of Europe in early 2016—in January we were there, and we got lots of signatures under the motion for resolution, it took us one year to launch the procedure. And you know why? Because the Russian officials tried to block it. They tried to influence the president; his name is Pedro Agramunt from Spain. And they were very successful. And it was a miracle that we managed to put through this procedure. I think it passed by one vote in March 2017. So that's a clear sign that they are really embarrassed, and they don't want these hearings to be held here today.

Secondly, your question about media coverage. First of all, there are official figures in the recent polls, and they show that 20 percent of Russians are not indifferent to what happened to my father and to his memory. That's a lot. They take into account this massive propaganda. And that's what I saw on the media. So regarding coverage, yesterday's event enjoyed substantial coverage in the Russian media and abroad. And also, of course, the still-existing independent media cover the case, and the fact that the case was not solved. And my third point is that for the third year, thousands of people in Moscow and in other Russian cities and in foreign cities, they took to the streets to commemorate my father—thousands of people. That's important.

Regarding your question, yes, my father sometimes mentioned that—he understood that the risks were really high. And he also talked about the possibility that he might be killed. But he was not that sure. He believed that he could have been put into prison. And this risk, he regarded as a material one. But he also talked about the possibility of murder, not only with me but also with the press. But I don't think that he regarded it as a material risk. He talked about this, nonetheless.

Mr. WICKER. Thank you.

Senator Cardin.

Mr. CARDIN. Well, let me thank all three of you for just powerful testimony. And we all understand that this is the Helsinki Commission, and every signatory state has signed onto the Helsinki Principles, and that gives every member state the right to question the conduct of every other member state. We have that obligation and responsibility.

So our objectives are to get Russia to do what's right, not for us to have to take action against Russia because they're doing what's wrong. So the purpose of the sanction law is for countries that do not do the responsible things. The Magnitsky law was passed because of the failure of the Russian authorities to bring the perpetrators of the tragedy against Sergei Magnitsky to justice. The Global Magnitsky Act applies universally to violations of human rights.

And we're not finished yet. Congress passed additional sanction authority, some of which is mandatory, against Russia in regards to its defense and intelligence sector because of their activities against other countries and other individuals. We have obtained information in regards to the oligarchs. There was a public release, but there's also private information that's being used, because we know they finance the corruption within Russia which allows Mr. Putin to be able to do what he does. We have also looked at the financing of sovereign debt, as to whether we can affect Russia as far as its banking activities are concerned. We're looking at the energy sector and what can we do against the energy sector. So we're not finished yet. I want to make that clear.

But I would like to get your view. How important is it to the cause of freedom in Russia the sanction activities that have been led by the United States Congress?

Mr. KARA-MURZA. Senator Cardin, thank you for this very important question, and thank you for all your work and all your efforts over the past now almost eight years since you first introduced the Magnitsky bill here to end the brazen impunity for human rights abusers.

As you know, Boris Nemtsov came here many times, not just here in Washington but here to Capitol Hill, to meet with members, including yourself, including the chairman of the commission, to discuss the importance of precisely this process. And his attitude to sanctions was—and he said it both privately and publicly—"don't touch the country, punish the scoundrels." That is a direct quote from Boris Nemtsov.

He viewed, as do I and as do many of our colleagues, that these sanctions should have a personal nature. Because it doesn't make much sense from our point of view to punish an entire country for the actions of a small, corrupt authoritarian clique sitting in the Kremlin. And as we all know very well, the current government of Russia, the regime of Vladimir Putin, is not a democratically elected government. If you read the reports from observers from OSCE and Council of Europe countries, we have not had a free and fair election in Russia since at least March of 2000.

So, in our view—and this was the brilliance of the principle behind the Magnitsky Act—this was a revolutionary principle, in our view, in international relations, that you actually assign responsibility for human rights abuses where that responsibility is due: to their perpetrators, to the people who are doing these things.

And, of course, the way it's so important and effective is because there is this fundamental hypocrisy, fundamental double standard at the heart of the Putin system of power, whereby the same people who violate and undermine and abuse the most basic norms of democratic society in Russia want to use the privileges and enjoy the privileges of democratic society in Western countries. They want to steal in Russia, but spend in the West. They want to send their kids to study in the West, open bank accounts in the West, buy real estate and luxury cars in the West. And the Magnitsky Act puts a stop to that. And we think it should, because on the part of the Putin regime and its officials and its oligarchs, this represents, as I mentioned, a massive hypocrisy. But on the part of Western countries who accept these people on their soil and in their banks, in my view that constitutes enabling—enabling of corruption and human rights abuse in Russia if you welcome those people on your soil.

And so that is why it was so phenomenally important when more than five years ago now the United States became the first country in the world to put down this principle, that those people who deny their own citizens the fruits of democracy will no longer be allowed to enjoy them for themselves and for their families. And we hope that this process continues. We hope that many more human rights abusers—there are only a few dozen, as of today, people designated under the Russia-specific Magnitsky Act as human rights abusers here in the United States. It's very important that it now includes both General Alexander Bastrykin and Ramzan Kadyrov. But there are many, many others, as you know well, who deserve to be on that list. And it's heartening to see more and more democracies adopt the same principle.

Last week I was in Copenhagen meeting members of the Danish Parliament, and we're hoping to convince them to do something similar, and there are other countries where they have those initiatives. And we hope that this law, the law that you authored, continues to be rigorously and fully implemented in the United States, and that those people who bear responsibility for human rights abuses will face some accountability for that.

Mr. CARDIN. I want you to know these bills were passed with strong bipartisan support. We have a very efficient and effective working relationship with the administration on the implementation of the Magnitsky sanctions. And the administration has been very open to information that we have made available, some of which has been provided to us by third-party sources. And we invite you to continue to supply us with information as to those individuals that may very well be considered for additional sanctions.

I do want to ask one more question if I might, Mr. Chairman, and that is, could you just tell us how is Mr. Nemtsov's murder handled by the Russian press? How did they handle the episode when it occurred, the trial, et cetera? You've indicated that it has a spin different than your facts. Could you just tell us how the Russian media has handled this?

Mr. KARA-MURZA. Thank you, Senator. That's a very important question. And I can give you the most recent example possible, and that is from yesterday. And yesterday when, as I mentioned earlier, the Russian state television channel, Rossiya 1, actually had a report on the unveiling of Boris Nemtsov Plaza here in Washington, the correspondent said that many of the speakers—and they included both senators and members of the House, including the chairman of the commission, Senator Wicker, who was with us yesterday—they did mention on the report that many of the speakers had called for holding those responsible who had committed this crime. And then they provided the comment: but those people are already being held responsible; they're all convicted and they were all sent to prison, and that is it.

And this is a classic substitution here, because of course what people, including Chairman Wicker, were talking about yesterday at the ceremony is about the need to identify and prosecute the organizers and masterminds of this crime, because it is not enough. And as Vadim said, we don't think all of the perpetrators even have been brought to justice. But none of the organizers or masterminds have. And any expert in basic criminology will tell you that you cannot consider a crime solved unless you have punished those who ordered and organized it, and General Bastrykin has declared this crime solved.

Mr. CARDIN. But does the state media raise the issues of additional investigations being suggested or needed?

Mr. KARA-MURZA. Absolutely not. According to them, this case is closed. This is done. Forget about this. They want to forget and move on. And as Vadim and Zhanna have mentioned, the only tools we have for now—until we have a normal and real justice system in our own country—the only tool we have are those international mechanisms that are available either through the Council of Europe, which have already been enacted, or through the OSCE, which we are hoping you could help us initiate.

And I want to make a very quick point to what you said earlier about the Magnitsky Act. On the day the U.S. House of Representatives passed the Magnitsky Act—this was November 16th, 2012, the third anniversary of the death of Sergei Magnitsky, and as you said it was passed with a huge bipartisan majority—Boris Nemtsov and I were sitting on the balcony, on the gallery there in the U.S. House of Representatives, watching how members of the House were voting on this, and Boris said something that I'm always going to remember. He said this law, the Magnitsky Act, is the most pro-Russian law ever passed in any foreign country, because it targets those people who abuse the rights of Russian citizens and who steal the money of Russian taxpayers.

Mr. WICKER. Senator Shaheen.

HON. JEANNE SHAHEEN, COMMISSIONER, COMMISSION ON SECURITY AND COOPERATION IN EUROPE

Mrs. SHAHEEN. Thank you, Mr. Chairman.

And thank you to each of you for being here and for your testimony.

To go back to that sort of effort to identify the people who are perpetrating human rights violations and who are stealing from the Russian people, one of the things that I'm sure you all would agree is that Vladimir Putin and his associates have amassed a tremendous amount of wealth that belongs to the Russian people that they're using for themselves. And I'm curious about what the reaction would be of those oligarchs and of Putin if information about what they have stolen is produced publicly. One of the benefits, I think, to the list of oligarchs that was produced as a result of our sanctions law is that it does hold people up and say: These are people who have made a lot of money through questionable means. How would people react to that, both those people who are being targeted as well as the Russian people—to doing that kind of a "name and shame" sort of thing?

Mr. KARA-MURZA. Thank you, Senator, for you question. Well, on this, we don't even need to guess, because we know the answer to your question. Almost a year ago now, in March of 2017, the Anti-Corruption Foundation, which is headed by Alexey Navalny, produced a report—an investigation, it was a video, in fact, detailing the secret financial empire of Russian Prime Minister Dmitry Medvedev, showing his yachts, his villas, his vineyard in Italy, a lot of sneaker shoes for some reason—that was a big point of discussion at the time. And of course, if you watched Russian state television, you would not hear a single word about this, needless to say. And yet, more than 20 million people in Russia watched that investigative video on YouTube. And tens of thousands went out to the streets to protest against this pervasive government corruption that is at the heart of the Putin system.

And they went to the streets despite the threat of arrests. And indeed, many arrests were made. Despite the threat of sackings or expulsions from universities, and all the pressure that was applied. This issue really angers people, because it's really obvious. I mean, people realize this is their money that is being stolen and used in this fashion, to buy some government official a vineyard in Italy or whatever else. And so this is an issue that is actually really high up in public attention. It's also an issue that is very scary for the regime. And of course, they're trying to hush it up as much as they can. But any efforts to shed light on that, and to shed light on instances of corruption but also on the involvement of some of these people in foreign financial dealings and the assets they hold abroad—this, I think, frankly, is one of the most effective things that can be done, because I don't think any people would like their money being stolen in such a brazen fashion by the people who are supposedly there to guard their interests.

But this is what these people are doing. They're stealing. They're stealing in Russia. And, again, they want to spend that stolen money in the West. So it is really important that the world's democracies put a stop to that practice.

Ms. NEMTSOVA. May I add something?

Mrs. SHAHEEN. Yes, please.

Ms. NEMTSOVA. I have a lot. It's a whole list of additions to what you have said. Now, I would like just to add on the last point about the Kremlin list you were talking about, as far as I understand.

People in Russia didn't get it. They didn't understand what was the reasoning behind this list, because some people appeared there who left Russia a decade ago. And they have nothing to do with Putin. Other people made their fortune not because they stole a lot of money—for example, Arkady Volozh who is the founder of Yandex. I am not advocating, but the reaction was like that.

What was the reasoning behind this list? Why were these people included and others were not—for example, Anatoly Chubais or the head of the central bank, Elvira Nabiullina. So it needs clarification, otherwise I don't know whether it was harmful for the oligarchs. But as far as I know from talking to some people from business circles, they were happy that everybody was included. So there were not only 5 or 10 people, but a whole list. But experts in Russia, they are lost with this Kremlin list and with this step, and they don't know what to expect.

And more broadly, I would like just to—your question, Mr. Cardin, was how sanctions bring democracy——

Mr. CARDIN. Before you do that, if Senator Shaheen would just yield for one moment, I couldn't agree with you more on the public list that was released by the administration on the oligarchs. It was a cut and paste of the *Forbes* list. There's also a classified list that we cannot talk about. And many of us are trying to get the administration to carry out the intent of our statute, which was to have a greater understanding about the corruption within Russia and the key players in that corruption, some of the oligarchs. So we are following up on it, but I just want to make it clear to you there was also a classified list that was filed that is much more granular than the list that was made public.

Mrs. SHAHEEN. And I think there was some question here in the United States, too, about the list that was released.

Ms. NEMTSOVA. I know. It was all over the world. And your question was about sanctions and democracy—how sanctions can bring democracy. And empirical evidence in Russia and in other countries show that these two things are not related to each other. And especially broad sanctions cannot lead to any transition or any change. And I fully agree with what Vladimir has already said about personal sanctions. They are, of course, very harmful. And people who are in power in Russia or wealthy people—they, of course, will try to do something not to be on this sanction list.

But we don't know the long-term influence of these personal sanctions because we don't know how much division they create among Putin's elite. Because this substantial divide could possibly facilitate change inside the elite. And we don't know, because we have a very closed system. And you just do things with your eyes shut sometimes. [Laughs.] Thank you.

Mrs. SHAHEEN. One of the things that I, and I think others in the United States, have found troubling has been President Trump's unwillingness to identify Mr. Putin as a human rights violator, to call him out for the interference that has happened in our elections, for some of his other activities, to raise the issue of human rights with him. What kind of a message does that send to the people of Russia, that the president of the United States has been unwilling to go after Mr. Putin for his human rights violations?

Mr. KARA-MURZA. Thank you, Senator, for your question. Well, I think if you look back on the 18 years—almost 19 years now— that Mr. Putin has been in power, we have unfortunately seen a tradition of U.S. presidents—of either party—sending messages that sometimes really fell far short of what they should have been—if you'll allow me to say so. I remember President Bush who looked into Mr. Putin's eyes and got a sense of his soul. I remember President Obama who declared a reset and praised Mr. Putin for the great work he had done on behalf of the Russian people. So, in a way, that's an unfortunate tradition that has existed for some time.

And it is very important that throughout all those years there was strong bipartisan leadership here in Congress, here on Capitol Hill, with initiatives such as the Magnitsky Act—leadership in favor of standing firm on values, standing firm on such issues as democracy, human rights, rule of law, countering corruption. And I think Congress—and, again, both parties in Congress—have played a very important role in keeping the whole of the United States Government faithful on those issues. And we hope that this good tradition of strong bipartisan leadership on democracy and human rights continues, and as part of this general context that this case—the Nemtsov assassination case—is also given the proper attention that it deserves.

Mrs. SHAHEEN. Thank you.

Ms. NEMTSOVA. May I add something about Trump, if you don't mind? I know that Russia was the only country where Trump enjoyed the highest rate of support before the presidential election. I think his rate of support was around 80 percent. Not a single European country had the same figure of support for Trump. And it's the same story with all American presidents, because of course Putin was strongly in favor of Mr. Trump. And afterwards, when this situation with Russia's meddling into the election started to unfold, the propaganda changed its focus, and now they do not praise Mr. Trump anymore. And it was the same story with Obama, because they were saying, like, Obama is the best choice, never McCain. Then Obama got elected, then he got into conflicts with Russia, and then he was portrayed as evil. So that's the same. I think that Trump will have the same image in Russia.

Mrs. SHAHEEN. Thank you.

Thank you, Mr. Chairman.

Mr. WICKER. I think we've gotten a lot into a brief hour. As I said, there will be a vote at 4:30, so let me just do this so we make sure we haven't omitted any really salient points.

Let me start with Mr. Prokhorov, and then just go down the table and see if there are words of summary or some follow-up points that need to be made to everyone within the sound of our voices this afternoon. Mr. Prokhorov.

Mr. PROKHOROV. Thank you so much.

First of all, I would like to come back to this idea about the importance of personal sanctions against those who violated human rights. By the way, it's a very, very dangerous activity in our country to support this idea. There are two persons from Russia who supported the adoption of Magnitsky Act: Mr. Boris Nemtsov, who was killed just near the Kremlin—it's impossible to be more near to the Kremlin than on the Bolshoi Moskvoretsky Bridge—and the second person is my friend, Vladimir Kara-Murza, who is also present here. He was poisoned twice. It's a very dangerous, but it's a very important activity.

And Boris Nemtsov, I remember that he often said that it's very important to pay attention to the reaction of the Russian authorities [to] some activities. For example, after the adoption of the Magnitsky Act, the reaction of the Russian authorities was hysterical. So it means that this process is quite powerful, and the influence of this Act is very, very high, and very, very important for us.

And as to this case, I could only repeat that for us it's very important because we have very, very few real legal tools to force our Russian authorities to make any real steps towards those who organized and sponsored this crime. And we hope the help from international organizations, such as Organization for Security and Cooperation in Europe, maybe it's possible to start the procedure of a special representative, a special rapporteur. We are devoted to this case because it's very important to pay attention and to ask questions of our authorities.

Thank you so much.

Mr. WICKER. Mr. Kara-Murza.

Mr. KARA-MURZA. Thank you, Mr. Chairman.

A couple years ago, Vyacheslav Volodin, who is now the speaker of the Duma—was then the deputy chief of staff at the Kremlin, Mr. Putin's deputy chief of staff—said on the record publicly a phrase, and I quote: "There's no Russia without Putin." There is nothing more insulting that I can think of to say about our country.

Unfortunately, too often some political leaders, experts, journalists in Western countries kind of implicitly accept that line, and blur the line between a country and a regime that misrules that country, and equates the whole of Russia with the Putin regime. Even on the level of language, even semantically—I know it may sound like a trivial point, but, people talk about Russian hacking, Russian aggression, Russian whatever, Russian abuses. That's not Russia. That's a small, authoritarian, unelected clique sitting in the Kremlin.

Boris Nemtsov was Russian. He loved Russia. He was a Russian patriot. He dedicated his life to a free and democratic Russia, and he gave his life for Russia to one day be free and democratic.

And so we would ask you, political leaders in Western democracies, both in North America and in Europe, to not equate Russia and the regime that is misruling it. And those thousands—tens of thousands of people who have been going out to the streets all across Russia in this past year to protest against the corruption and the abuses and the sham elections and all the rest of it, everything that's associated with the current regime, that's Russia too. And I think it's very important for our colleagues and counterparts in the democratic world to remember that.

And I have absolutely no doubt, just as Boris was certain about this, that one day we will have a government in Russia that will both respect the rights of its own citizens and rule of law and democratic principles, and that will live at peace with its neighbors, and that will behave as a responsible member of the international community. And as we were saying yesterday at the unveiling ceremony, whatever people in the Kremlin think today, I have absolutely no doubt that there will come a time when the Russian state is proud that our embassy in Washington is standing on a street that is named after Boris Nemtsov.

Mr. WICKER. Thank you very much.

And if you have some follow-up comments, Ms. Nemtsova, you're welcome to say those at this point. Happily, our co-chairman of the commission has arrived, and I'm going to turn the gavel over to him so that Senator Shaheen and I can go and vote. But at this point you're recognized to make any follow-up comments that you'd like to.

Ms. NEMTSOVA. Thank you. I will try to keep it short, and it's really, really short just to sum up what has already been said.

I read on Facebook—these are not my words—and it said: "Boris Nemtsov is becoming as important for Russia as Andrei Sakharov." And that's true. He is a young symbol and his importance is growing. Everybody in Russia and outside Russia admits this important fact. And he's the only one who can bring people together, different people who have different convictions or some different views on various things. And taking these two things into account, it's a shame that we don't have an investigation, and we have to put pressure to have a full and transparent investigation into my father's murder. Thank you.

Mr. WICKER. Thank you.

Co-Chairman Smith, you are recognized.

HON. CHRIS SMITH, CO-CHAIRMAN, COMMISSION ON SECURITY AND COOPERATION IN EUROPE

Mr. SMITH. Thank you very much, Mr. Chairman. Thank you. Good to see you, my good friend.

I'm sorry I was late and I missed your testimonies. I was actually chairing a hearing on Zimbabwe. I chair the Africa, Global Health, Global Human Rights Committee, so I deeply apologize to you because I could not be here to hear all of your statements.

And, Zhanna, thank you for your bravery in coming here. Your dad would certainly be proud that you are here. He was a colleague, and we all deeply respected him for his commitment to the rule of law, to human rights. So I just want to say that there's a true solidarity here.

This commission, I've been on it since my second term in 1983, and we have always raised the issues with what was then the Soviet Union and the East Bloc, and now Russia of course, because the day where democracy has broken out and flourished is still a hope, it's not a reality—particularly under Mr. Putin.

You know, just a couple of questions because, again, I came late, so I missed the flow of what has already gone before me. But the Magnitsky Act was a huge breakthrough, in my opinion, and I think it's shared by many of my colleagues—to finally say we will hold individuals accountable. The Global Magnitsky, in like manner, is now a very useful tool against repressive regimes.

I'm wondering if there's something more that we need to be doing, as a country. We have an OSCE Parliamentary Assembly meeting coming up in July, and we will meet with our Russian counterparts, or at least attempt to. And certainly we will raise this issue with them. You know, impunity becomes worse when these assassinations and killings go uninvestigated. And who calls the shots? Those people don't go to prison.

So I would ask you for your recommendations to us, what we might do, and also, about the elections issue vis-à-vis Putin, Trump, whatever happened in the last election, I think, has chilled our ability. I can't get a visa to go to Russia. I was hoping to go a number of times. One time I met with the ambassador. It was all set, we thought. And because of the Magnitsky Act and the fact that I was the House sponsor of the Magnitsky Act, it precluded my getting a visa.

During the worst years of the Soviet Union, I was able to get a visa. I went to Perm Camp 35 with Frank Wolf in the mid to late 1980s, where Sharansky had been and so many other great political prisoners. And yet now many of us find ourselves unable to even travel to Moscow. And frankly, if I could, I would. And I'll make a renewed request to go. And I would raise your dad's case, believe me, if we could get there.

So we are in a very bad place, I think, with regards to Russia. But again, your recommendations on what you think we could do, and especially the OSCE Parliamentary Assembly, which will be in July?

Mr. KARA-MURZA. Thank you, Co-Chairman Smith, and thank you for your efforts and your leadership over the many years on issues of human rights and democracy, including with regard to our country.

And, first of all, I think the fact that you have been placed under a travel ban by the current Kremlin regime, you should consider that as a badge of honor, as I know many people who have been placed under similar circumstances do. I know it's frustrating. It's inconvenient. But it is a badge of honor.

But I think it also illustrates a wider picture, that some of the things in Russia today compare, in terms of domestic repression, to what it was in the late Soviet times, the time that you began to serve in this House. For example, even if we're talking about the numbers of political prisoners, even those are becoming very similar.

In 1975, when Andrei Sakharov wrote his Nobel lecture, which he was not allowed to go to Oslo to deliver, he listed in it by name 126 prisoners of conscience in the Soviet Union. Today, according to the Memorial Human Rights Center, according to the latest report, we have 117 political prisoners in the Russian Federation. And that's a very conservative estimate. The number is probably much higher. But this is done using very restrictive criteria under Resolution 1900 of the Parliamentary Assembly of the Council of Europe. And even by that standard, we have more than 100 people.

There are many other similarities. You know, all the main television channels serve as propaganda tools for the state. Parliament is a rubber stamp. We have no free and fair elections. But in some ways the situation is worse, because back then, back in the early 1980s, the period you just referred to, the most prominent political dissidents in Russia or the Soviet Union were in prison, in internal confinement or in forced exile—Sakharov, Solzhenitsyn, Bukovsky.

Today the most prominent political dissident in Russia is dead. Three years ago yesterday, he was killed. Boris Nemtsov was killed on the bridge in front of the Kremlin. And so I think you're right to raise that comparison.

And there's also another difference between that time and the time we're living in today. You know, when members of the Soviet Politburo were doing all of those things they were doing, putting people in prison for political reasons, censoring media and all the rest of it—they, the members of the Soviet Politburo, did not keep their money in Western banks. They didn't send their children to study in Western schools. They didn't buy real estate or luxury cars or yachts in Western democratic countries. These guys do.

The oligarchs and the officials in the Putin regime do that. The same people who undermine and abuse and violate the most basic norms of democratic society in Russia want to use the privileges and the opportunities of democratic society in Western countries. They want to steal in Russia and spend in the West. And the Magnitsky Act, of which you were one of the co-sponsors in the House more than five years ago now, is an absolutely crucial and indispensable tool that puts—or at least begins to put—an end to this impunity and introduces some sort of personal measure of responsibility and accountability for these people in the absence of a real justice system in Russia.

As we were discussing earlier, frankly, the Magnitsky Act is a pale substitute for real justice. I mean, if you kill or torture someone, your punishment should not be that you're not allowed to buy a house in Miami Beach. It should be that you're tried and convicted if you're guilty. But at least it's something. At least it's some sort of personal responsibility.

So I want to thank you for your leadership on the Magnitsky Act and express my hope that this process, the implementation of the Magnitsky Act, now also the Global Magnitsky Act, because human rights are universal, so accountability for violating human rights should also be universal. We hope that process continues.

And on your point about the specific recommendations, we may actually—all three of us, we may actually see you in Berlin in July for the summer meeting of the OSCE Parliamentary Assembly, because one of the things we're really hoping to try to do—and this is the reason it's so important for all of us to be here today—is to engage international oversight mechanisms over the official Russian investigation into the assassination of Boris Nemtsov, because we feel that that process has been inadequate, that it has been politically restricted.

And today, more than three years after the leader of the Russian opposition was killed, none of the organizers or masterminds of this crime have been brought to justice or even identified. And there are many, many other problems that will now be part of this hearing record, because we have raised many of those issues in detail. I don't want to take up more of your time, but we are happy, especially Vadim, to address the legal details in this.

So the only really effective tool, perhaps the only tool that we have available to us in this situation, is to engage international oversight. And thankfully, Russia is a member of international organizations that are founded on these principles of human rights and the rule of law—the Council of Europe. And there we already have an international oversight mechanism effected through the appointment of a special rapporteur at the Parliamentary Assembly of the Council of Europe. He was appointed last year with a mandate to review all the aspects of the Nemtsov case and shed light on the constraints and the limitations and the problems and the inadequacies.

So now we are hoping, with your help, to initiate a similar procedure within the auspices of the Organization for Security and Cooperation in Europe and the Parliamentary Assembly of the Organization for Security and Cooperation in Europe; be it with the appointment of a special representative, be it with a public hearing that will start some kind of an oversight process, maybe the Moscow Mechanism.

These are the things that you know everything about and I don't need to tell you anything about those. But it is really important to have some sort of oversight and to shed some sort of light internationally and to expose those problems and those restrictions and those limits, because as far as the Russian authorities are concerned, the Nemtsov case is solved and closed. They've had a trial of some of the perpetrators. They've sentenced them to prison. And according to them, this is done. Move on. Forget about it. Turn the page.

We do not think that that is OK. We do not think that it's OK without identifying the motive, which they haven't done, without identifying the organizers and masterminds, which they haven't done, to say that this case is closed. And we are counting on international organizations. We are counting on our partners in these international organizations. And frankly, we are counting on you to engage this oversight and to make sure that there is no impunity for those who had ordered, organized and carried out the most high-profile political assassination in modern Russia.

Ms. NEMTSOVA. Vladimir has already said everything, but my specific recommendation is that it's very easy to figure out what to do with the Russian authorities. You probably are aware what they are afraid of most. They're afraid of the sunshine. That means that they want to cover up everything. They want to end public debate on those issues which are sensitive for the Russian political leadership.

And my father's case is one of the sensitive issues. And that's why it's important to bring it to the sunshine, to speak about it in the media especially, not only with your Russian counterparts, but also when the media outlets are there. So to talk about that publicly with your Russian counterparts, that's important, and that's embarrassing for them.

And Vladimir raised a very important question, and now I'm talking not only on behalf of my father, but also on behalf of the Boris Nemtsov Foundation for Freedom which we founded in 2015 in Germany—and Vladimir Kara-Murza is chairman of the board of trustees, so we have a program to support political prisoners and political refugees from Russia.

It's a small program, but what we learned out of our experience is that if you create a lot of public resonance, a lot of public attention in the media—a lot of coverage—that helps a lot of those political refugees, and that's the only reason why some of them were released in Russia, including the latest case with Yury Dmitriev. He was released because of this unprecedented public attention, and it was the case with Ali Feruz, a journalist from Uzbekistan who our immigration service finally allowed to leave Russia, and now he is in Germany. They wanted to extradite him to Uzbekistan, and he would have been killed there—tortured, imprisoned and killed. So if you create this great media coverage and public debate, it helps, and it's proven.

Mr. SMITH. Let me ask you—for years I've been going to the UN Human Rights Council as a place where you get this much satisfaction because very often rogue nations sit on the Human Rights Council. The great reform that was supposed to take place didn't, but I do think it still provides a venue where human rights issues can be discussed, but consequences are often minimal. But it is an opportunity.

And Russia's Universal Periodic Review comes up in May of 2018, just a few months from now. I'm wondering if there has been any outreach? We certainly will be in contact with our team—our diplomatic team, starting with the Secretary of State, Rex Tillerson, Nikki Haley, and others who are a part of that effort.

And I'm wondering if you have sought to get the issue of Boris Nemtsov discussed at the Human Rights Council, as Russia goes through that review of their record—or lack of good record—on human rights?

And secondly, has there been any positive consequences or contact with Prince Zeid bin Ra'ad Zeid al-Hussein, the Jordanian High Commissioner for Human Rights, whom I've met with in the past? I've raised human rights issues with him, a lot of Russian human rights issues. Has he shown any sense that, on an extraordinarily high-profile case that speaks volumes for all the others, but in and of itself it's enough—has he shown any willingness to engage when it comes to your dad?

Ms. NEMTSOVA. So as far as I know, we didn't have a chance to talk about this case at the Human Rights Council of the United Nations, and I was at the United Nations, and I took a part last year in the Geneva Summit on Human Rights that is under the umbrella of the United Nations. And Vladimir went there this time, so we raised this issue, we talked about my father's case at the summit, but I learned—I talked to some people from the U.N., I learned that it would be very difficult to bring this issue today at United Nations Human Rights Council right now because of its composition.

Mr. SMITH. But I don't think we shouldn't do it for lack of a positive result. As you mentioned, media coverage, bringing the case in a very forceful way with facts and documentation could put the Russians in the hot seat. They're going to have to give an accounting for their human rights record, and members of that council can ask tough questions. And there are a number of European friends and partners that are on that council. We could ask tough questions as well.

Ms. NEMTSOVA. Yes, that would be absolutely great if we can make connections with them. So far I haven't made any connections.

Mr. SMITH. What we'll do is put together this hearing record, which again lays out the case I think very powerfully—because I did see your earlier statements, but I did not hear the oral testimony because of my own hearing on Zimbabwe.

But I think we should do a letter to Prince Zeid, ask him to use his human rights apparatus—and he's got a huge bureaucracy that could delve into your father's assassination, and also ask member states on the Human Rights Council to raise it robustly with the Russians as they appear.

Mr. KARA-MURZA. Mr. Co-Chairman, if I can briefly add—first of all, thank you for the suggestion, and you are absolutely right in that the basic human rights, of which the right to life is perhaps the most important one—which is the right that has been violated in the case of Boris Nemtsov—is of course protected by the Universal Declaration of Human Rights, so it does fall under the purview of the United Nations. You are absolutely right.

And as Zhanna said, I was in Geneva last week for a forum, but also to meet with some of the diplomats from the democratic nations that are members of the U.N. Human Rights Council, including Canada, the U.S., European Union countries.

Unfortunately, as you know very well, some of the members of the U.N. Human Rights Council have themselves been some of the worst human rights abusers, and that continues to be the case. But we're very grateful to you for that suggestion, and I think it's a very good idea to actually try to raise this case within the framework of the U.N. and with the help of the U.N. High Commissioner for Human Rights, whom you have mentioned. And we would be grateful for your assistance and leadership on that.

And we also will continue the efforts within the framework of the Council of Europe and the Organization for Security and Cooperation in Europe, and of course the difference with those organizations, as opposed to the U.N. Human Rights Council, is that the vast majority of member states in those organizations are countries that respect democracy and the rule of law themselves.

Mr. SMITH. That's right.

Mr. KARA-MURZA. And so we really count on our international partners in this case to hold the current Russian Government to account on our country's international obligations on matters of human rights and rule of law under the European Convention on Human Rights, under the OSCE Copenhagen document, under the OSCE Moscow document, which is probably my personal favorite of all the international treaties, because that document states very clearly, black on white, that matters relating to human rights, fundamental freedoms, and the rule of law cannot be dismissed as, quote, unquote, "internal affairs" of that or other member state, and that they are subject to international concern, and that they are subject to concern by other member states. And we hope that our partners in the OSCE, including the United States, exercise their right to express that concern and exercise their ability to raise those issues in the international framework.

Mr. SMITH. Well, I can guarantee—we'll do a letter too and contact not only our own delegation, but also countries that I think— as you pointed out—you know, do have a firm grasp of what due process, rule of law, human rights really are all about because, again, forget about the rogue nations. They'll do anything but be asking hard questions.

So that, during that Universal Periodic Review, Russia can give an accounting and hopefully be held to account, and maybe it could lead to some breakthrough somehow. And of course, at the OSCE Parliamentary Assembly and at the OSCE itself, we'll press it very hard. But we'll get on that right away. You have provided us with good, actionable information to take it even further, so we're very grateful for that.

Mr. PROKHOROV. Mr. Co-Chairman, as the lawyer for Zhanna Nemtsova—and by the way, I've been a lawyer of Boris Nemtsov himself for 14 years—and for us, it is absolutely clear that there is an imperative need to draw international attention to this issue. We have a very, very limited choice of legal tools in our country, in the framework of our legal system unfortunately.

And I hope that maybe one of the most effective legal mechanisms from the international point of view is Organization for Security and Cooperation in Europe. If I am not mistaken, there will be some meetings, some conference in July——

Mr. SMITH. Yes.

Mr. PROKHOROV.——in Berlin.

Mr. SMITH. That's right.

Mr. PROKHOROV. And so it would be great if it would be possible to start the procedure of a special representative, something similar to the special rapporteur in the framework of the Parliamentary Assembly. But it seems to me that the Russian authorities pay much more attention to the framework of the Organization for Security and Cooperation in Europe, and where the United States is also a member. And so for us it's very important—to initiate the procedure of a special representative—maybe if it would be possible in these summer meetings.

Mr. SMITH. I can promise you we'll try. There are just a small number of special reps with the OSCE PA. I'm one of them. I do it on combating human trafficking. Our ranking member, Ben Cardin, does it on behalf of combating anti-Semitism—so, you know, there are just a few, but we will try. I think it's a very, very good idea.

Tied up in the whole case of Boris Nemtsov would be the impunity, the assassination, that is just in a league of its own. It just tells the whole story because it chills other people from speaking out boldly because that could be them. And so for Boris himself, we need a full accounting and for all parties responsible to be held to account, total transparency, and no more of this opaqueness and cover up, but it also has a great impact on democracy in Russia itself, at the Duma and everywhere else.

So it is well worth the effort, and we'll do it. And again, I think we need to use every tool in the tool box. That's why I brought up the Human Rights Council and, not surprisingly, you are already talking to people there. We'll do a letter to Prince Zeid. I have met with him, like I said before, and very often, his office is—well, the pressure should not be that they don't look at things because a member state is on the Security Council and a very powerful one at that. Injustice is injustice wherever it is committed.

Is there anything else you would like to add—because I know one of you do have a plane to catch at five.

Mr. KARA-MURZA. We've covered pretty much everything, Mr. Co-Chairman. We'll be really grateful for your leadership at the Parliamentary Assembly of the OSCE at the summer session, where we're hoping to be, too, so maybe we could do a public event or a hearing, and if you need any assistance or any help from our side, from the side of the family, friends and colleagues of Boris Nemtsov, you will have our full cooperation in these matters.

Mr. SMITH. Well, you know, one thing that we might consider—a side event with you there might be helpful as well, to alert the parliamentarians about this case. There are a lot of people who probably have read about it and seen it somewhere but, you know, didn't really have the depth that you bring to bear on that while we're in Berlin.

Mr. KARA-MURZA. Absolutely, and then an important aspect that Vadim has mentioned——

Mr. SMITH. Yes.

Mr. KARA-MURZA.——that, as you know, for the last two years, the official Russian delegation has been boycotting the Parliamentary Assembly of the Council of Europe—they're not actually turning up there. They do turn up, as you know, to the OSCE Parliamentary Assembly meetings, so that's something you would actually be able to state to their face.

Mr. SMITH. They often show up just to push back on Ukraine and the illegal taking of Crimea.

Mr. KARA-MURZA. Well then, how about actually making them answer for something they should answer to, and I think that would be a very good idea to try to do something in Berlin, and I think I can speak for all three of us when I say that if such a side event happens, we would be happy to take part, and turn up, and do whatever is necessary to try to move this forward.

Mr. SMITH. Thank you.

Mr. KARA-MURZA. Thank you.

Mr. SMITH. Thank you for your courage, tenacity, your friendship, your love for your dad.

We will look forward to following up on all of these things, and we will put those letters together right away—you know, to the president, to Tillerson, and—because that Universal Periodic Review is coming up in May, so it's right around the corner. And I think that will be a good place to really engage, in addition to all the others.

The hearing is adjourned, and thank you very much.

[Whereupon, at 5:03 p.m., the hearing ended.]

APPENDIX

PREPARED STATEMENT OF HON. ROGER WICKER, CHAIRMAN,
COMMISSION ON SECURITY AND COOPERATION IN EUROPE

The Commission will come to order, and good afternoon to everybody.

We are turning our attention in today's hearing to the loss of one of Russia's great democratic reformers, Boris Nemtsov, who was gunned down within sight of the Kremlin three years ago yesterday. Although the triggermen were apprehended and tried for their crime, the masterminds behind it have never been identified.

Our witnesses today are people who knew Boris Nemtsov well. I stood beside them yesterday in the ceremony to rename a section of Wisconsin Avenue as Boris Nemtsov Plaza. I am also very pleased that this hearing will focus on the legacy of Boris Nemtsov as Russians prepare to cast their votes in another presidential election next month. We are honored to have his daughter, Ms. Zhanna Nemtsova, join us to reflect on her father's work and the prospects for realizing his dream of a free and democratic Russia.

Ms. Nemtsova is joined by somebody who is no stranger to me, the Helsinki Commission, nor the halls of Congress, thanks to his tireless work promoting democracy in Russia. Mr. Vladimir Kara-Murza knows better than almost anybody about the intense—and all too often lethal—pressure being applied to brave Russians, like him and Boris Nemtsov, who engage in opposition politics. Vladimir directed the documentary film *Nemtsov*, a truly remarkable tribute to Boris that opened in Nizhny Novgorod and was screened in Moscow, St. Petersburg, and Washington, where many people in this room had a chance to see it.

We are also very fortunate to have Mr. Vadim Prokhorov, the lawyer for the Nemtsov family, who has worked for years now to see the masterminds of this heinous act brought to justice.

As I mentioned, yesterday our witnesses participated in the naming ceremony for the Boris Nemtsov Plaza. As an American, I am proud Washington has held the very first official commemoration of Boris Nemtsov anywhere in the world. The Russian people should know that we will continue to build legislative monuments to their heroes here until those stone monuments can be built in Russia.

Let me also offer a word about the posters on display at the front of the room. They serve as a reminder that brave Russians have gathered on a regular basis to ask for justice for Boris Nemtsov. The photo of these flowers at the site of his murder could have been taken virtually any day in the past three years. Despite being removed every day, the flowers are always replaced the next day by the many people who revere the memory of Boris Nemtsov. I think these people deserve to be recognized for their devotion to democracy in Russia and for their dedication to honoring one of Russia's great democratic leaders.

We hope to accomplish two things at today's hearing.

First, we want to remind all members of Congress and the American public that the democratic freedoms we take for granted have been under siege in Russia, at least since Vladimir Putin was first elected president in 2000. Until an election is declared "free and fair" in Russia by credible international observers, we will need to revisit this theme, letting Russians know they have not been forgotten by their friends.

Secondly, with our witnesses' assistance, we would like to evaluate the prospects for delivering justice. Holding the perpetrators accountable for Boris Nemtsov's murder is an important first step toward providing the security that Russians will need to exercise their democratic rights. And since justice, at the moment, seems impossible to find inside Russia, I would like our witnesses to tell us what the international community, specifically the OSCE, can do to bring justice for Boris Nemtsov outside of Russia.

I am convinced now more than ever that a Russia that allows for full freedom of expression and free and fair elections will be a place where all Russians can prosper. Those improvements would also make Russia a much better neighbor, going a long way toward promoting peace and security in the entire Eurasian region.

We have a lot to discuss, so I'd like to yield to Senator Cardin.

PREPARED STATEMENT OF HON. BENJAMIN L. CARDIN, RANKING
MEMBER, COMMISSION ON SECURITY AND COOPERATION IN EUROPE

Mr. Chairman, thank you for holding this important hearing on
slain Russian opposition leader Boris Nemtsov's legacy.

It is still hard for me to believe that just three years ago Boris
Nemtsov was assassinated just steps outside the Kremlin. Having
led a fruitful career in government, Mr. Nemtsov refused to cooper-
ate with Vladimir Putin's system of authoritarianism unlike many
of his peers. Instead, he worked tirelessly to defend the fundamental rights of Russian citizens and expose corruption within the
Putin regime. I am honored to have worked with him on some of
the Helsinki Commission initiatives. He was vital in our work to
pass the Magnitsky Act, which has become one of our greatest tools
in fighting corruption in Russia. Mr. Nemtsov was truly a great
man of courage and conviction. It was exactly this courage that led
to his untimely assassination. Mr. Nemtsov's murder was shocking
and outrageous even in a country where violence against human
rights and democratic activists has become routine. Mr. Nemtsov's
death was a major loss to the Russian people and all those who
fight for democracy around the world.

This past summer five of the men involved in Mr. Nemtsov's
murder were convicted by Russian courts. One of these men was
Zaur Dadayev, the gunman who shot four bullets into Mr.
Nemtsov's back. It is worth noting that Mr. Dadayev served as a
commander of the Chechen security forces under Chechen leader
Razman Kadyrov, a close associate of Vladimir Putin. This past
summer's trial left many questions unanswered. While Mr.
Dadayev and his accomplices have been punished, the masterminds
behind the assassination have not been served justice.

Since rising to power in 2000, Putin has ruled Russia with an
iron fist. Under Putin, democracy and human rights have greatly
suffered. Beyond Mr. Nemtsov, many others who have spoken up
against the Putin regime have been killed under dubious circumstances, including investigative journalist Anna Politkovskaya,
human rights activist Natalya Estemirova, and Umar Israilov, just
to name a few. In addition, our witness Mr. Vladimir Kara-Murza
has been subject to two poisoning attempts. I've repeatedly stated
that Russia is violating each and every principle of the Helsinki
Final Act's guiding principles. It is more important now more than
ever that we work to protect fundamental human rights in Russia.

I recall how Boris joined me for a screening of "Justice for
Sergei" in November 2010, and almost immediately after was assaulted at the airport upon returning to Russia. His bravery and
perseverance will remain etched in my memory forever, he stood
for all Russians having a say in their government, a truly fantastic
retail politician, in the best sense of the word.

The Russian government is committed to fighting Mr. Nemtsov's
legacy. I, too, am saddened by the reports that every night government workers steal the flowers from Mr. Nemtsov's unofficial me-

morial located at the spot he was killed. Yet Mr. Nemtsov's supporters, everyday Russians who believe in a brighter future for their country, are not dissuaded and replace the stolen flowers every day. Even though Mr. Nemtsov's voice may have been silenced by a gunman in Moscow, his words will never be forgotten. I will do all in my power to ensure his legacy reverberates throughout the world.

I yield my time to Mr. Smith.

PREPARED STATEMENT OF HON. CHRIS SMITH, CO-CHAIRMAN,
COMMISSION ON SECURITY AND COOPERATION IN EUROPE

Good morning, and thank you Chairman Wicker for convening this exceptional hearing.

Yesterday, we commemorated the block of Wisconsin Avenue in front of the Russian Embassy as *Boris Nemtsov Plaza*. With this gesture, we hope to signal to those Russians in the tireless pursuit of real and lasting democracy in Russia, that their friends in the United States have not abandoned them. It was a quite the ceremony: remarkable, timely, and something I will not soon forget.

We would be remiss then if we did not take advantage of the occasion to remember and discuss Mr. Nemtsov's work, his legacy and the possibility of bringing those responsible for his assassination to justice. We are fortunate to be joined by an esteemed panel of witnesses: Zhanna Nemtsova, his daughter; Vadim Prokhorov, the family lawyer; and Vladimir Kara-Murza, the chairman of the Boris Nemtsov Foundation for Freedom, and no stranger to the Commission. Your thoughts and perspectives are invaluable to the Commission, and again, we thank you for joining us this afternoon.

Mr. Nemtsov was no common politician. As a democratic activist, he wanted to break through the corruption and authoritarianism that has gripped Russia since Vladimir Putin took power in 2000. The human rights abuses suffered by the people of Russia and those outside of its borders are tragic and unacceptable. But, Mr. Nemtsov imagined a greater Russia, a Russia made free by an open press, a judicial system governed by the rule of law and not the whim of despots, and a Russia guided by the premise that Russians ought to have a say in the way their government operates. He died a man of great honor and courage. May we all endeavor to act on our convictions as he did.

Mr. Nemtsov was not only a politician. He was Zhanna's father, and for many of us here, our friend and colleague. We may never know who masterminded his murder, but it is without doubt that he was slain for his political beliefs.

Although Boris was taken from us three years ago, the outrages against democratic activists continue today. Just recently Russian authorities charged the Leader of "New Opposition," Mark Galperin, with public incitement to extremist actions by means of the internet. Calls to join mass public demonstrations or to change the government, without a direct indication that this should be done by means of violence, are not unlawful and cannot be considered criminal offences. As we consider Boris Nemtsov's legacy today, let us not forget that democratic activists like Mark Galperin are under extreme pressure from the Russian authorities.

The assassination of this remarkable leader also speaks to the need for historic justice. Time, even years, doesn't lessen the need for accountability in crimes like this, and addressing them is necessary for society to truly move on. This was a key lesson I took away from my work on Northern Ireland.

Boris was killed mere steps from the Kremlin. I have stood outside the Kremlin myself and have taken in the incredible power and size of that fortress. In many ways, the Kremlin is as much a fortress for Putin, cloistering him behind yes men and thieves.

Wresting Russia from his grasp may seem as daunting a task as scaling the Kremlin walls but our friend, Mr. Nemtsov believed not only that it could be done, but that it must.

I'd like to take this time to again, thank our esteemed witnesses and our friends and guests for joining us here today. While the Putin regime did everything in its power to push Mr. Nemtsov to the margins of Russian political life, he will not be on the margins of our minds and our hearts.

We have a lot to cover in a short amount of time, so Mr. Chairman, I yield my time.

○